Schofield & Sims

The World

Ages 4-5

Understanding the World

Get Set Early Years

Name

Introduction

The **Get Set** activity books are full of fun activities that help you to reinforce at home the learning that your child is doing at school.

This activity book is about **The World**. It focuses on developing your child's understanding of animals, habitats, environments, materials, weather and seasons. The book falls within the curriculum area of Understanding the world in the Early Years Foundation Stage (EYFS) framework and is supported by two other activity books for Understanding the world: **People** and **Technology**.

It is recommended that your child starts this activity book at the beginning of the Reception year, completing one or two pages at a time over the course of the year. They should complete pages 4 to 11 in Term 1, pages 12 to 19 in Term 2 and pages 20 to 29 in Term 3. As your child works through the book, the tasks will gradually become more challenging, requiring more reading, writing and numeracy skills, helping to prepare your child for the more formal style of learning that begins in Key Stage 1.

It is worth remembering, however, that children develop and learn in different ways and at different rates, especially at this young age, and you may prefer to work through the books at your child's own pace. The activity books may also be suitable for older or younger children, depending on ability.

Before beginning each activity, read the instructions aloud to your child. Discuss what they can see in the pictures and what they have to do to complete the activity. The friendly illustrations will inspire lots of conversation and give plenty of opportunities for mark-making – an important first step when starting to write.

At the back of the book you will find **Notes for parents and carers**, with helpful guidance relating to each page of the activity book. For each topic, there is a **Teaching tip**, which explains how best to support your child as they complete the activities, **Key vocabulary**, for you to model and encourage your child to use themselves, and a practical **Extension activity**, for you to explore the topic further with your child in a real-life context.

These notes help you to get the most out of the activity books and to support and enhance your child's learning. When working through the activities, don't worry too much about your child 'getting it right'. The emphasis should instead be on 'having a go' and taking the time to enjoy exploring new topics and ideas together.

Published by **Schofield & Sims Ltd**,
7 Mariner Court, Wakefield, West Yorkshire WF4 3FL, UK
Telephone 01484 607080
www.schofieldandsims.co.uk

This edition copyright © Schofield & Sims Ltd, 2018
First published in 2018
Fifth impression 2022

Authors: **Sophie Le Marchand and Sarah Reddaway**
Sophie Le Marchand and Sarah Reddaway have asserted their moral rights under the Copyright, Designs and Patents Act, 1988, to be identified as the authors of this work.

British Library Cataloguing in Publication Data
A catalogue record for this book is available from the British Library.

All rights reserved. No part of this publication may be reproduced, stored in a retrieval system, or transmitted in any form or by any means, electronic, mechanical, photocopying, recording or otherwise, without either the prior permission of the publisher or a licence permitting restricted copying in the United Kingdom issued by the Copyright Licensing Agency Ltd.

Design by **Oxford Designers & Illustrators Ltd**
Cover illustration by **Conor Rawson**
Printed in the UK by **Page Bros (Norwich) Ltd**

ISBN 978 07217 1448 6

Contents

Farm animals 4

Animals around the world 5

Animal babies 6

Humans 7

How humans grow 8

Footprints 9

Animal habitats 10

Mini-beasts 11

Plants 12

Trees 13

In the country 14

In the city 15

Objects 16

Materials 17

Patterns around us 18

Animal patterns 19

Weather 20

Dressing for the weather 21

Seasons 22

Seasonal colours and words 23

Hot and cold 24

Hot and cold places 25

At the beach 26

Holidays 27

Flags around the world 28

Languages around the world 29

Notes for parents and carers 30

Farm animals

Find the animal pairs.

Draw over the dotted lines and colour the animals.

Get Set Understanding the World

Animals around the world

Find and colour the animals.

Draw lines to match the animal's head to its body.

The World

Animal babies

Draw a ring around the right baby for each animal.

Draw some ducklings beside the ducks.

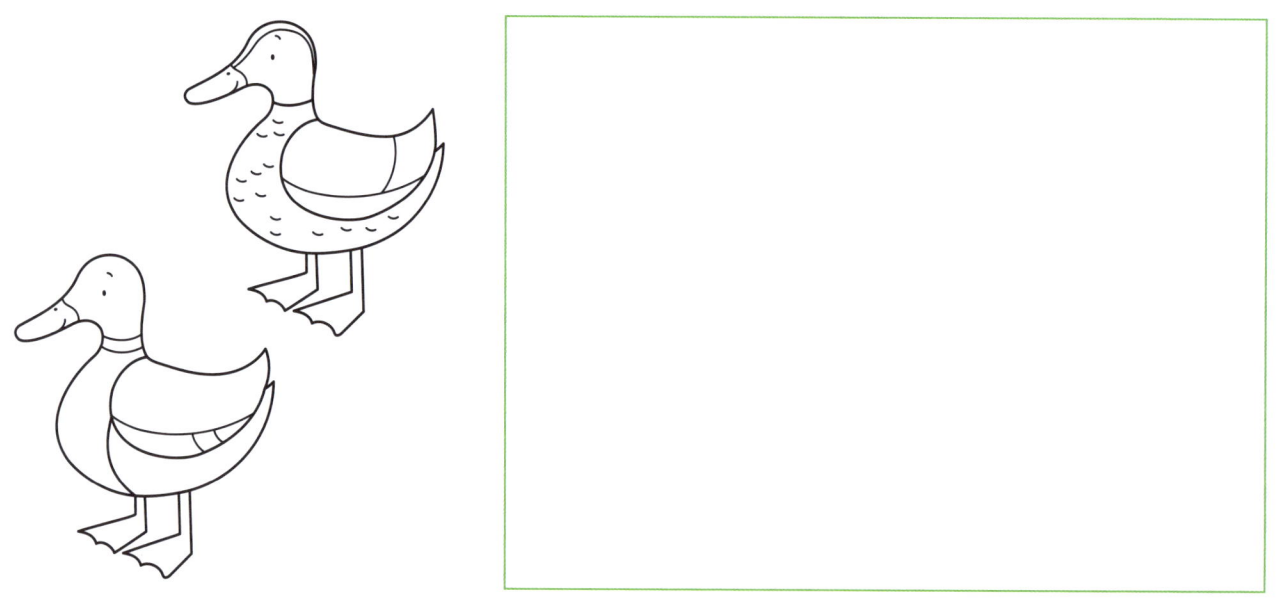

Humans

Describe the different people. Draw over the dotted parts of the pictures.

Spot the 5 differences between the skeleton pictures. Draw a ring around each one.

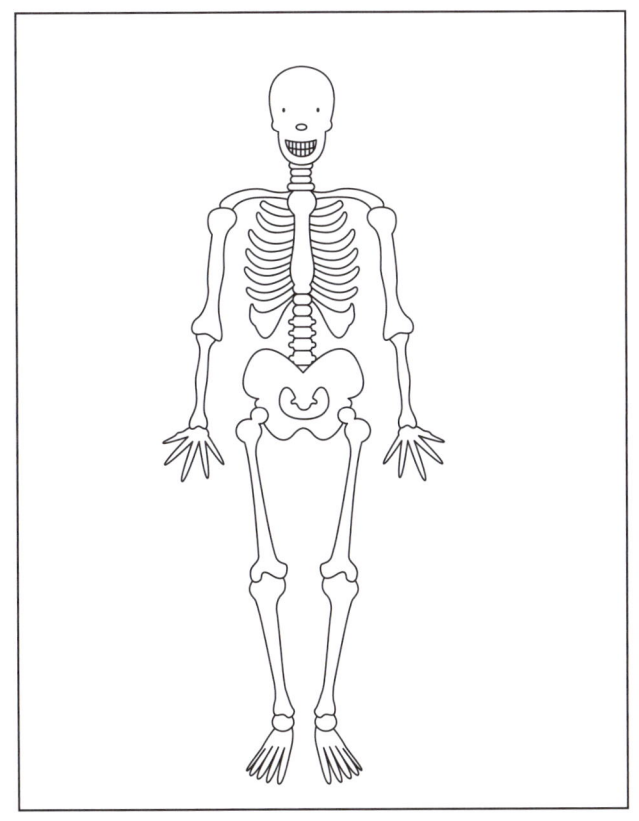
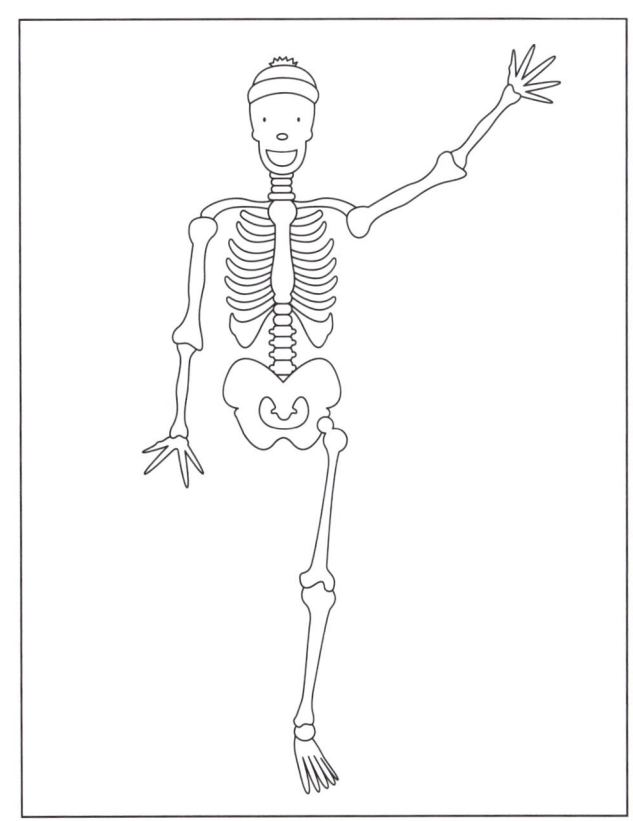

How humans grow

Draw a ring around all the things that a baby needs.

Draw a baby to show the youngest age.

Footprints

Follow the footprint trail to help the man find his dog.

Draw lines to match the footprints to their owners.

  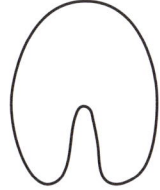 

Animal habitats

Draw over the wiggly lines to help the animals find their homes.

Colour all the animals in each habitat. Draw a ring around the animals that are away from their usual home.

Get Set Understanding the World

Mini-beasts

Draw the other half of the mini-beasts to finish the pictures.

Find 10 mini-beasts. Draw a ring around each one.

Plants

Draw over the dotted flower and colour it. Name the parts of the flower.

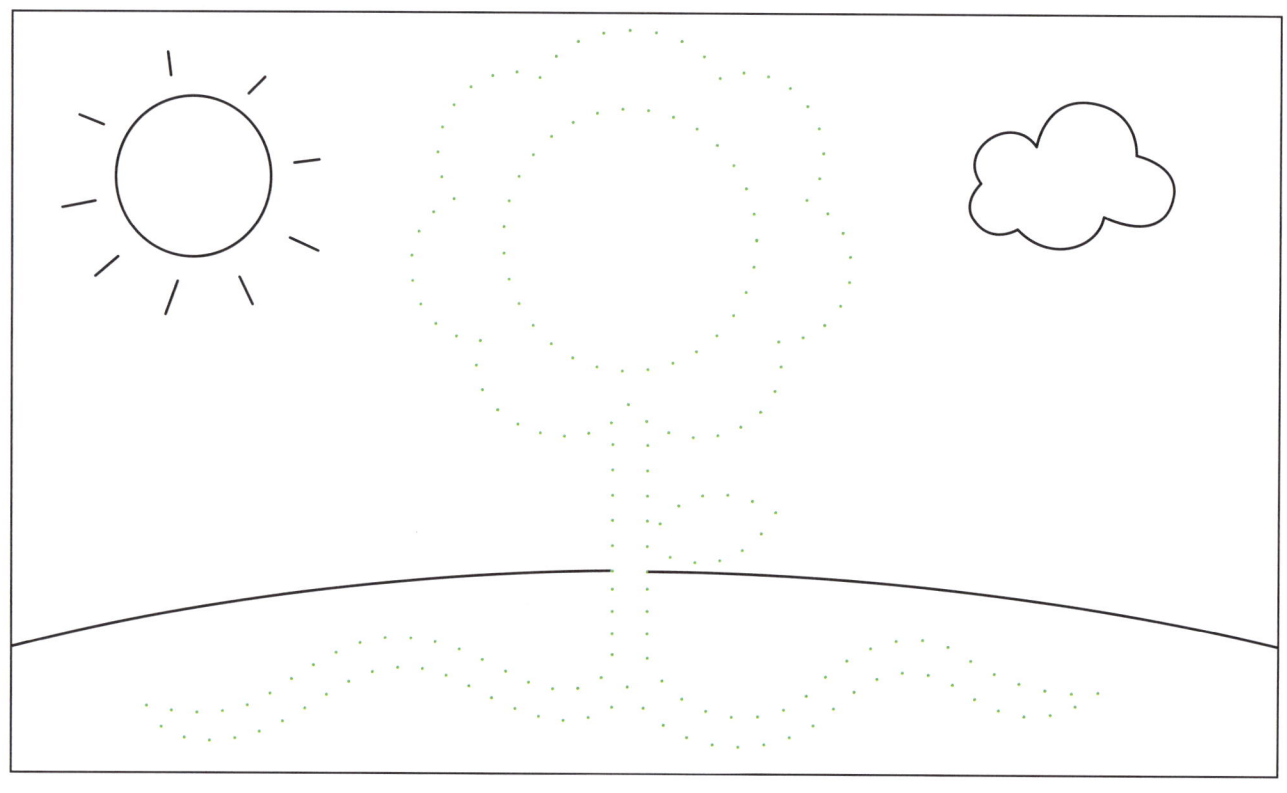

Tick the things that a flower needs so it can grow.

Trees

Draw a ring around all the things that grow on trees.

Order the pictures to show the life cycle of the apple tree. Write a number from 1 to 4 beside each picture.

The World

In the country

Spot the 5 differences between the countryside pictures. Draw a ring around each one.

Colour all the things that a farmer needs.

In the city

Draw a line on the road to find the way to school.

Draw over the dotted shapes on the road signs.

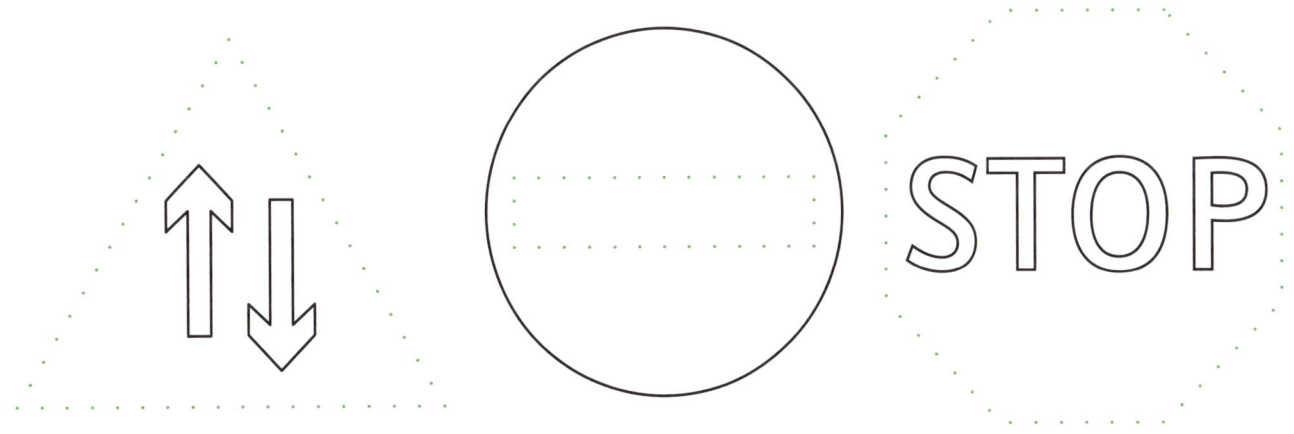

The World

Objects

Draw lines to match the objects to how we use them.

Draw the other half of the objects to finish the pictures.

Materials

Colour the objects made of hard materials yellow and the objects made of soft materials green.

Draw a ring around the objects that are not made out of wood.

Patterns around us

Draw over the patterns on the T-shirt. Draw your own T-shirt patterns.

Colour the patterns in the picture.

Animal patterns

Colour the butterfly pattern by numbers.

1 brown   2 red   3 green
4 blue   5 yellow

Draw lines to match the patterns to the animals.

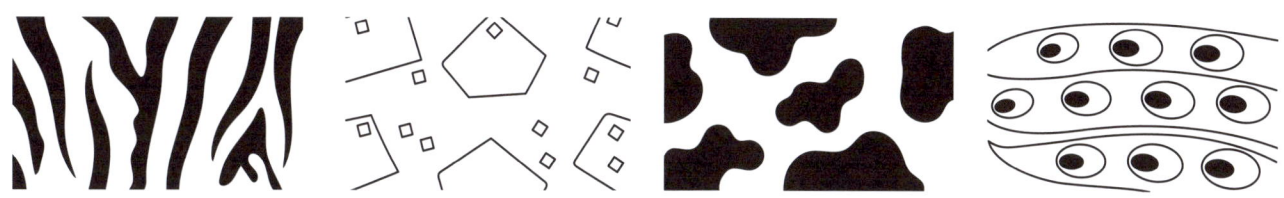

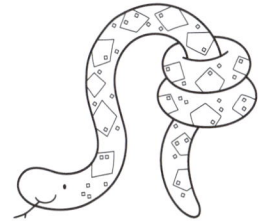

The World

Weather

Join the dots of the weather pictures. Trace the weather words.

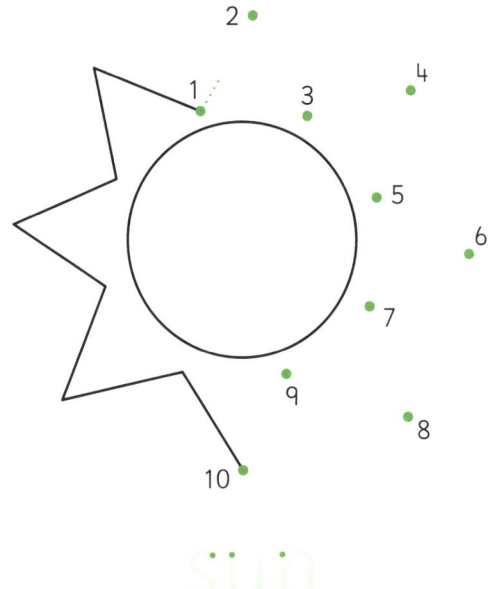
sun

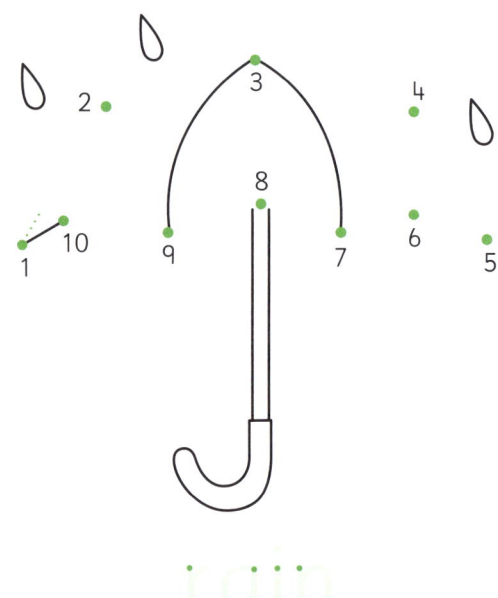
rain

Spot the 5 differences between the windy pictures. Draw a ring around each one.

Dressing for the weather

Draw a ring around the odd ones out.

Draw the weather that the children are dressed for.

The World

Seasons

Draw over the dotted lines to finish the pictures. Read the season words.

spring

summer

autumn

winter

Follow the wiggly lines to find the right season.

Seasonal colours and words

Colour the tree for each season. Choose the colours carefully.

spring

summer

autumn

winter

Find the seasonal words in the word search.

rain
sun
tree
spring
winter

a	u	t	w	g	c	j
n	s	s	i	p	a	i
r	a	i	n	f	d	m
x	i	n	t	r	e	e
s	u	n	e	c	g	a
p	s	p	r	i	n	g

The World

Hot and cold

Colour the hot objects red and the cold objects blue.

Trace or write 'hot' or 'cold' under each picture.

Hot and cold places

Draw a ring around the odd ones out.

Draw lines to match the animals to their habitat.

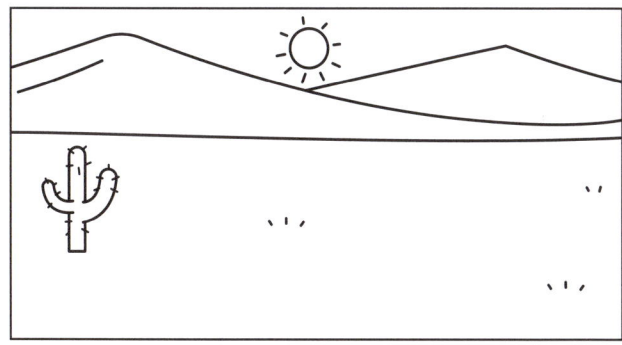
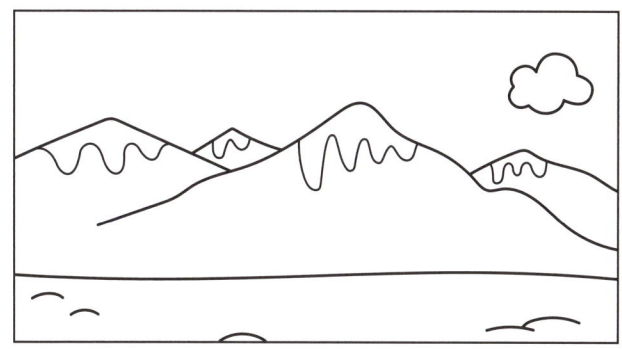

The World

At the beach

Draw what comes next in each seaside pattern.

Draw a ring around all the dangers at the seaside.

Holidays

Colour all the summer holiday objects.

Write the missing words, draw yourself, and tick a box to finish the passport.

Name: _____

From: _____

Boy ☐   Girl ☐

The World

Flags around the world

Colour the flags by numbers.

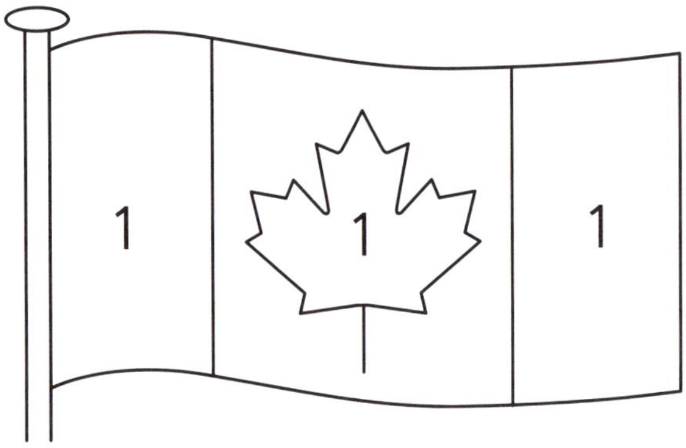

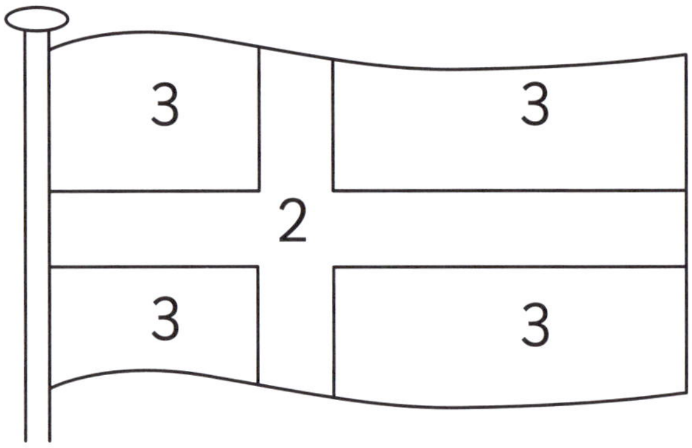

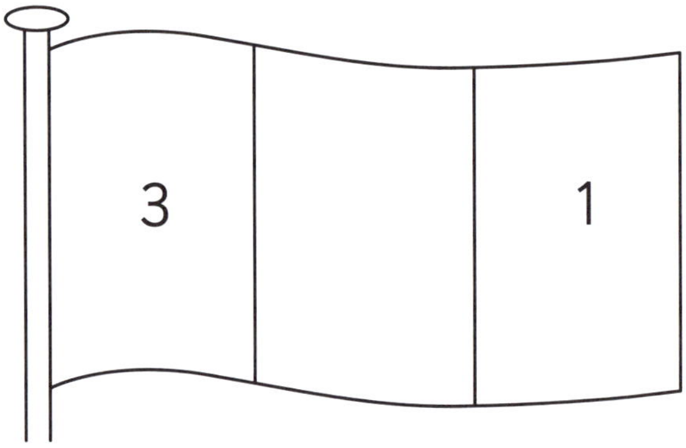

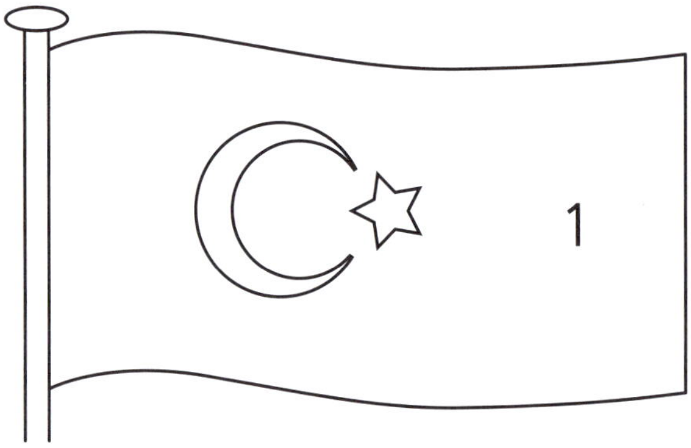

1 red   2 yellow   3 blue

Design your own flag.

Languages around the world

Say the words that mean 'hello'.

hello

ni hao

hola

namaste

bonjour

konnichiwa

Trace the number words in English. Try to count from 1 to 5 in Spanish.

1   one   uno
2   two   dos
3   three   tres
4   four   cuatro
5   five   cinco

Notes for parents and carers

Topic	Teaching tip	Key vocabulary	Extension activity
Farm animals page 4	Help your child to choose appropriate colours for the animals. Discuss the different colours a sheep's coat can be.	animal, cow, horse, sheep, goat, hen	Take your child to visit a farm.
Animals around the world page 5	Encourage your child to talk about the features of each head and tail that they are matching.	snake, monkey, tiger, shark, elephant, crocodile	Watch a wildlife documentary together and discuss where the animals come from.
Animal babies page 6	Notice together how some baby animals have the same name (for example, baby cows and baby elephants are both called 'calves').	lamb, foal, piglet, puppy, calf, cub	Make models together of an animal family using play dough or a similar alternative.
Humans page 7	Give clues to guide your child in the right direction if they need help to spot the differences, rather than show them the answer.	person, human, age, body, skeleton, bone	Use black paper and white chalk to create a skeleton drawing together.
How humans grow page 8	Encourage your child to explain why a baby does or does not need each item, to pick up on any misunderstandings.	baby, child, adult, life cycle, grow, change	Show your child a family photo album and see how everybody has changed over time.
Footprints page 9	Ask your child to explain why they think each footprint matches or not.	footprint, barefoot, paw, hoof, claw, trail	Help your child to make a painted family footprint collage. Discuss who has the biggest and smallest footprints.
Animal habitats page 10	Ask your child where each animal lives. Talk together about different habitats and what they are like.	live, habitat, sea, farm, crab, octopus	Help your child to make a shoe box environment for the farm or sea.
Mini-beasts page 11	Explain that 'mini-beast' is the collective name for many small animals.	mini-beast, spider, ant, butterfly, ladybird, snail	With your child, gather mini-beasts on a mini-beast hunt. Can your child name them all?
Plants page 12	Discuss with your child the things a plant needs to grow.	flower, seed, soil, root, stem, petal	Plant some cress seeds with your child and ask them to draw pictures to show the changes as the seeds grow.
Trees page 13	Ask your child to explain what changes they notice in the sequence of the growing tree.	tree, trunk, branch, leaf, fruit, acorn	Ask your child to make a list, in pictures, of everything they can think of that grows on trees.
In the country page 14	Give clues to guide your child in the right direction if they need help to spot the differences, rather than show them the answer.	countryside, nature, village, environment, wildlife, tractor	Take your child on a country walk to collect countryside objects, such as pine cones, grass, leaves and sticks.
In the city page 15	Ask your child to name each building that they pass in the maze on the way to the school.	city, building, busy, noisy, traffic, sign	Help your child to make a map of a 'built environment'. You could find and cut out pictures of city buildings together.
Objects page 16	Encourage your child to look carefully and keep to the right size when completing the objects.	object, size, shape, use, make, collect	Help your child to make a time capsule and put some special objects inside it.
Materials page 17	Talk to your child about what a carpenter does. Explain that wood comes from trees.	man-made, natural, wood, metal, fabric, plastic	Challenge your child to find some 'squishy' and some 'transparent' items at home.

Topic	Teaching tip	Key vocabulary	Extension activity
Patterns around us page 18	Give clues to guide your child if they need help to spot the pattern, rather than point the patterns out.	pattern, stripe, spot, zigzag, brick, tile	Do crayon rubbings together of different patterns that your child finds around them (for example, wood, brick or tiles).
Animal patterns page 19	You may need to help your child to understand the key by marking the colours beside each number.	wing, print, patch, skin, fur, feather	Ask your child to create an animal with patterned fur, using a variety of arts and crafts resources.
Weather page 20	Remind your child of the numbers 1–10 by counting together before completing the dot-to-dot. You could use a number line to help.	weather, rain, cloud, snow, wind, sun	Ask your child to create a rainbow using paints or materials. Ask them to name all the colours.
Dressing for the weather page 21	Make sure that your child has grasped the weather words from the previous page before moving on to more difficult vocabulary.	sleet, hail, fog, storm, drizzle, rainbow	Help your child to design an outfit for a sunny or snowy day, choosing and cutting out different clothes from catalogues.
Seasons page 22	Read the season words aloud with your child, as they may find them difficult to read for themselves – 'autumn' is particularly tricky.	season, spring, summer, autumn, winter, year	Look at a calendar together and talk about months and seasons. Your child could try to write the season by each month.
Seasonal colours and words page 23	Encourage your child to look for the first letter of each word in the word search. You could help them with the other letters if needed.	bud, blossom, bare, fall, bright, dark	Help your child to make a collage of their favourite season using magazine or other cuttings and natural objects.
Hot and cold page 24	Help your child form their letters when writing, starting from the right place and moving in the right direction.	temperature, hot, cold, ice, melt, fire	With your child, make and freeze your own ice lollies.
Hot and cold places page 25	Use a globe or world map to show where hot and cold countries are. Explain the equator as an invisible line where the sun is hottest.	world, North Pole, South Pole, equator, desert, climate	Give your child cotton wool and arts and craft resources to create a picture of a snow scene, including some animals that live there.
At the beach page 26	Guide your child with clues to spot the patterns if needed. You could also use a clapping rhythm or say the objects out loud.	seaside, sand, sea creature, cliff, safety, danger	Ask your child to prepare and present a mini show using props, to illustrate how we can be safe at the seaside.
Holidays page 27	Encourage your child to take their time on the passport, adding extra details such as eyebrows and eyelashes.	holiday, travel, ticket, passport, suitcase, adventure	With your child, go on a role-play holiday to a place of their choice.
Flags around the world page 28	Talk to your child about which country each flag is from. Find the countries on a globe or world map.	flag, country, France, Canada, Turkey, United Kingdom	Help your child to make a flag of the country they are from.
Languages around the world page 29	Read the foreign language words and numbers aloud for your child to copy.	English, Spanish, French, Chinese, Hindi, Japanese	Challenge your child to count back from five to one in a language of their choice.

The World

Schofield&Sims

Help children to become school-ready with **Get Set Early Years**, an engaging cross-curricular programme to bridge the gap between play and formal learning.

Developed by experienced practitioners and based on the Early Years Foundation Stage framework, **Get Set Early Years** is designed to build confidence, encourage curiosity and foster a love of learning.

- exciting and motivating activities to support classroom teaching
- friendly illustrations that children can enjoy colouring in
- key vocabulary for each topic area, providing opportunities to create a rich language environment
- notes and tips for parents and carers to help you delve further into each topic

Get Set Understanding the World: The World immerses children in their surroundings, exploring the similarities and differences between places, objects, materials and living things. This book covers topics such as animals, mini-beasts, plants, habitats, weather, environments and holidays.

Discover the other **Get Set** activity books:

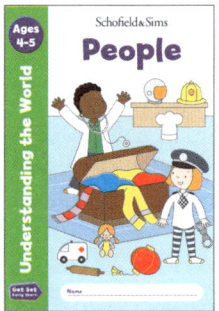

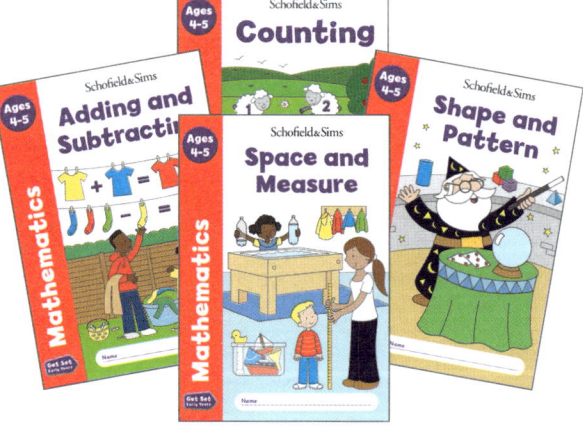

ISBN 978-07217-1448-6

MIX
Paper from responsible sources
FSC® C023114

ISBN 978 07217 1448 6
Early Years
Age range 4–5 years
£4.95 (Retail price)

For further information and to place your order visit www.schofieldandsims.co.uk or telephone 01484 607080